SUCCULENTS

SUCCULENTS

AN ILLUSTRATED GUIDE TO VARIETIES, CULTIVATION AND CARE, WITH
STEP-BY-STEP INSTRUCTIONS AND OVER 145 STUNNING PHOTOGRAPHS

Terry Hewitt

Photography by Peter Anderson

southwater

This edition is published by Southwater
an imprint of Anness Publishing Ltd
info@anness.com
www.southwaterbooks.com
www.annesspublishing.com

If you like the images in this book and would like to investigate
using them for publishing, promotions or advertising, please visit
our website www.practicalpictures.com for more information.

A CIP catalogue record for this book is available from the British Library.

Publisher: Joanna Lorenz
Editor: Margaret Malone
Designer: Julie Francis
Production Controller: Ben Worley

PUBLISHER'S NOTE

■ HALF TITLE PAGE
Crassula 'Morgan's Pink'
■ FRONTISPIECE
Euphorbia horrida
■ TITLE PAGE
Dinteranthus microsperus
ssp. *puberulus*

■ LEFT
Lampranthus haworthii
■ OPPOSITE LEFT
Dudleya hassei
■ OPPOSITE RIGHT
Aeonium haworthii

Contents

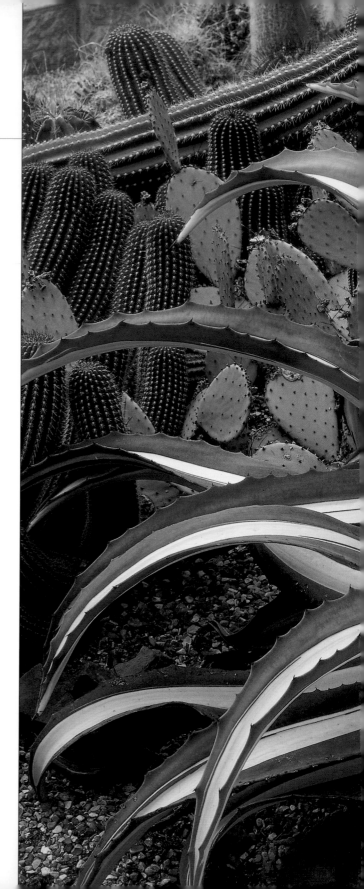

Introduction

There is a vast range of different succulent plants in an infinite variety of shapes, sizes and colours. Some groups are cultivated for their flowers, while many are grown for their shape and form. Some are very small and slow-growing, needing just a 5cm (2in) pot, while others are large and bizarre. There are the unusual small stone plants (*Lithops* and *Conophytum*), the small and large, succulent-leafed members of the Crassulaceae family, the climbing vines like the wax flower (*Hoya*), the large rosettes of the *Agave* and *Aloe*, the globular to tall-growing, spiny spurges (*Euphorbia*) and, of course, the amazing range of cacti, to name just a few. No matter how long you have been collecting, there are always new and fascinating succulents to catch your eye.

■ RIGHT

The majestic *Agave*, such as this *A. americana mediopicta alba*, make handsome feature plants for both patios and summer bedding or landscaping.

What is a succulent?

trees and bushes have overcome this problem by going into a state of dormancy in unfavourable conditions, while some of the shorter plants survive because of their storage organs – bulbs, corms or tubers.

In areas with little rainfall, apart from the rapid-growing annuals, many plants adapt by growing slowly, and conserving as much moisture as possible to see them through periods of drought. These plants are said to be 'succulent'. They can store moisture in three ways, by having fleshy or swollen roots, stems or leaves.

Many succulents come from dry, inhospitable areas where there is little competition for space from other faster-growing groups of perennials. These succulents occur in many different plant families, few being devoted solely to succulents. A brief introduction to these plants will help the reader understand them better, making cultivation and coping with their requirements much easier. Many problems can be solved using

Nature is very clever at adapting life forms to fit into their surroundings. Even in areas which would be completely hostile to most fauna and flora, different creatures and plants have adapted to fill a niche.

Plants need food, water, light and a certain temperature range to grow well. When food and water are abundant, the growth is fast and lush.

When water is not available for many months, plants can shrivel and die. Nature has, to some degree, overcome this problem by making many plants annual in their growth patterns – seed germinating, growing, flowering and setting seed before dying in the dry periods. Most annuals tend to be lower-growing, few becoming large bushes. Some

■ RIGHT
The unusual shape of the leaves of
this *Echeveria* 'Topsy Turvy' makes
it very distinctive.

normal gardening techniques, noting
that these plants need less water than
normal, and mostly object to very
low temperatures.

Many succulents are found in
deserts, that is, areas that have less
than 25cm (10in) of rain a year,
and many use the shade of stones or
boulders to get established. Others
can be found close to water courses,
above or below ground. Some small
succulents rely on the shade from
dead annual plants to give them
protection during the hottest months
of the year. Like most land masses,
desert areas are quite diverse. Some
are winter rainfall areas, and others
receive most water in summer. Some
of the maritime regions can be greatly
affected by cold Antarctic tidal
currents, as on the west coast of
Africa and South America.

The habitats for succulents can
therefore be quite varied, which
affects the way the plants grow.
Most of the plants normally found
in cultivation are summer-growing,
but some prefer to grow through the
winter, becoming dormant in late
spring when the weather warms
up. They do very little until the
temperature drops again in autumn.

Many plants have adapted to their
own particular habitat. Often lower-
growing forms are found in windy
areas, taller and more bushy plants in
damper areas. A large proportion of
the succulents in cultivation are from
Africa and Europe, the exception
being the cacti which are all natives
of the Americas. Both these land
masses cover similar latitudes, and it
is possible to see how different groups
of plants in different areas have
evolved similar forms. In Africa, the
spurge family (Euphorbiaceae) has
over 1,200 succulent species, many of
which resemble the cacti of the new
world. Likewise, the *Aeonium* from
the Canary Islands are very similar in
shape to the *Echeveria* of Mexico.

■ LEFT
Aeonium haworthii is one of the most
attractive bush-forming *Aeonium*s. Its
hemispherical mounded shape produces
many cream flowers in spring.

History

As most succulent plants occur naturally in the wild their history goes back thousands of years, before records were kept. The ancient Egyptians, Greeks and Romans knew of the healing properties of the *Aloe* several thousand years BC.

Most early documents and folklore mention succulents only in relation to their medicinal uses. In Africa, many succulents are used in traditional medicine, although very little has been actually recorded, most knowledge being passed by word of mouth. We know that some of the plants that produce underground storage organs are eaten, or first have

■ ABOVE
The milky sap of some spurges is used to make a lethal poison to tip darts, arrows and spears and also as a substitute for rubber.

their poisons removed before being ingested. The poisonous properties of the spurge family have been known for a long time. Local tribesmen throw branches of the plant into water-holes to poison them; when wild animals drink there, they are easier to kill. The same juice will stun fish, making them easier to catch.

Even in the UK there are about three species of native succulent, the most popular being the white-flowered stonecrop (*Sedum*), which has been used decoratively as a garden plant. In fact in the mountain regions of Europe there are many species of *Sedum* and *Sempervivum*. As far back as the 1st century AD *Sempervivum* are recorded as being used to ward off evil spirits. On a more practical note, from the northern parts of South America to the southern parts of North America, the fibres of the *Agave* were used to make ropes long before this group became popular as bedding plants in warmer areas.

Botanical expeditions

A large proportion of the succulent plants collected today come from Africa, and the first record of these plants from southern Africa is in the mid-17th century. As the popularity

■ ABOVE
Scientific research at the end of the 20th century led to the discovery of the anti-inflammatory drug cortisone, extracted from the large caudexes of the African *Testudinaria elephantipes*.

of plants increased so did the expeditions, and there were a great many of these expeditions in the latter half of the 18th century. The Royal Botanic Garden at Kew sent Francis Masson on its first botanical expedition to South Africa in 1772. He gathered over 100 different succulent plants, mostly of the Euphorbiaceae and Aizoaceae families and Stapeliad group.

Since that time there have been countless botanical expeditions to all corners of the world. New plants are always being discovered, even from areas often explored before.

Succulent plant groups

The succulent plant groups are varied in both form and size. Some genera have very large and small species. Other genera have a wide range of differing forms, making it difficult to be precise about the characteristics. However, the succulents can be loosely split into five main groups.

Stem succulents

One of the main groups of stem succulents is the cacti. Amongst the other succulents, the main stem

■ LEFT
The thickened fleshy leaves of many bushy succulents, such as this *Kalanchoe aff. marmorata*, store moisture to carry the plants through periods of drought.

■ ABOVE
Euphorbia fructosa. Similar environmental forces in Africa and America have resulted in many spurges resembling the cacti.

succulents include the Euphorbiaceae, many of which resemble cacti, and the Stapeliad group which has recently undergone many name changes and has mainly short, soft, finger-like stems, and can be quite difficult to grow. Other stem succulents include the tree *Sedum*, *S. frutescens* and *S. oxypetalum*, and many of the *Tylecodon* (formerly the stem succulent *Cotyledon*).

This group also includes the caudiciform succulents, a name originally coined for plants with swollen stems and/or roots, making large, swollen lumps. They include such plants as elephant's foot (*Testudinaria*), with its large, swollen,

hemispherical woody base from which the vines arise. Many such caudiciform have fairly short growing seasons, reverting to lumps for the rest of the year. In the main, each caudiciform has its own individual growing requirements.

Bushy leaf succulents

This large group of plants are much more like ordinary plants, but with swollen or thickened leaves. Most are not so particular in their requirements, and tolerate both over-cultivation and neglect. Most prefer a bright situation, but not necessarily full sun. The Crassulaceae family is

■ BELOW
Aloe distans. The swollen-leafed rosettes of the genus *Aloe* can be large or small, many being almost stemless.

■ BELOW
Haworthia cuspidata variegata. The swollen rosettes of *Haworthia* are often protected from the full sun under bushes.

group have coloured leaves, often blue, purple or bronze, and various shades of green. The different kinds of *Aeonium* from the Canary Islands mostly have rosettes of green leaves, but some species have these rosettes eventually on tall stems.

The many *Sempervivum*, from northern Africa and the mountains of Europe are almost the equivalent of the Mexican *Echeveria*, having small, hardy rosettes of colourful leaves, sometimes quite hairy. This group probably has the most attractive leaves if they are judged solely on colour.

■ BELOW
Echeveria lilacina. Many of the short colourful rosettes of *Echeveria* tend to close in periods of drought to conserve moisture.

the main one in this group with plants such as *Kalanchoe, Aeonium* and *Cotyledon,* with some from the Aizoaceae family (*Lampranthus* and *Drosanthemum*) and some from the *Aloe.*

Rosette-leaf succulents

This is another main group of succulents. Many grow in stemless or very short-stemmed rosettes. The Crassulaceae family provides us with the *Echeveria* group, the *Aeonium, Sempervivum* and *Adromischus,* and the old Liliaceae family (now divided up) with plants such as *Aloe, Haworthia* and *Gasteria.* Some of these plants are very robust, and tolerate long periods of drought with their often thick and chunky leaves. Many of the *Echeveria*

■ BELOW
Lithops lesliei. Known as living stones, *Lithops* grow in late spring, become semi-dormant in summer and flower in autumn.

Leaf succulents

Into this group fit all those plants, often quite diminutive, composed of little more than a few swollen leaves. The largest group is the Aizoaceae family, with plants such as the stone plants (*Lithops*) actually being a pair of swollen, united leaves. Many of the plants in this group have a short growing period, rapidly storing water in the wet season and slowly drawing on their reserves in the leaves to survive until the next wet season. This means some of the plants have different growing periods from the norm, which can be a problem for the new collector. Because these plants are so adapted to their unusual habitats they also tend to have fairly specific needs, and dislike poor cultivation and watering at the wrong time of year.

Root succulents

Most of the plants in this group have fairly specialized requirements, and are not often available in garden centres. Apart from some bulb-like species such as the knitting plant or climbing onion (*Bowiea*) and some tuberous *Ceropegia*, like heart vine (*C. woodii*), many are challenging to grow, showing little tolerance to overwatering or poor cultivation. Some of the specialist plants include many species in the cucumber and geranium families. The other plants are often in small groups of their own, showing little affinity to other groups of plants.

■ BELOW
Bowiea volubilis bulb. Although often cultivated above ground, the large onion-like bulb of *Bowiea* grows better when buried. The long climbing stem is produced in summer.

Indoor cultivation

Many plant families contain species which have adapted to areas with drier climates than those tolerated by typical garden plants. A proportion from more temperate areas are succulent and have thickened leaves, trunks or roots to carry them through periods of drought.

These attributes make succulent plants ideal for cultivation indoors, or in a greenhouse, as they enjoy a warm, dry atmosphere and will tolerate periods of neglect. If you are fortunate enough to live in a frost-free area, many succulents will make ideal garden plants, and there are some that are popular as summer bedding, such as the rosette-forming kinds of *Echeveria*.

Choosing the right plant

Succulent plants make ideal house plants because they enjoy the atmosphere in modern, centrally heated houses. These conditions are often unsuitable for many of the more popular house plants. As succulents are so diverse in the wild there are some to suit most bright positions, although not necessarily full sun. Many of the Crassulaceae family are quite happy on a bright, sheltered windowsill, for they dislike

■ RIGHT
A small collection of succulents growing in a porch. When choosing plants, take advantage of the wonderful diversity of shapes and colours among succulents.

full sun all day. On the other hand, many Aizoaceae prefer plenty of sun and do best in a sunny position. Some climbing plants, such as *Ceropegia*, *Hoya* and *Stephanotis*, also make good house plants and do very well in a bright room.

Many of the larger plants make good feature plants indoors, the most popular being the money plant (*Crassula ovata*). Although it will do best in full sun, it tolerates slightly darker conditions, but is then unlikely to produce winter flowers. Some of the newer introductions are rapidly gaining popularity as more exotic house plants. Some are large and do best in permanently warm conditions in full sun. The Madagascar palm (*Pachypodium lamerei*) was almost unobtainable

20 years ago but now is often available in garden centres. The desert rose (*Adenium obesum*) has also been appearing lately as a house plant. Although it can be difficult and temperamental in a greenhouse due to its high temperature requirements, it makes an ideal house plant for a warm, sunny windowsill.

There are also a number of succulents which, because of their rambling or trailing habit, are ideal for indoor hanging baskets. The trailing species *Kalanchoe* 'Tessa', with its orange-tipped scarlet bells in early spring, is popular, as is *K. pumila* with its small, grey-white farinose (powdery) leaves on long, trailing stems and small, delicate pink flowers in spring. Another popular house plant is string of beads (*Kleinia*

■ RIGHT
Many of the Bromeliad family, such as this rosette-forming urn plant (right), are semi-succulent and can complement a group, such as here with these *Echeveria* (left).

rowleyana) with its green, bead-like leaves on long, trailing stems.

Many of the smaller and slower-growing plants can be grouped in one container to make an indoor garden. As some succulents need water at different times of year only compatible plants should be put together. Often these will be closely related and found in similar terrain in the wild, such as the *Haworthia* and *Gasteria*. Although they are basically rosette-shaped plants, there is a wide variety of leaf shapes, textures and colours.

■ ABOVE
The softer lines of many of the leafy succulents, such as these *Crassula* and *Kalanchoe,* make them ideal for most bright living areas.

A collection of *Lithops* or *Conophytum* makes an attractive display when planted up into a container, interspersed with rocks and stones. Choosing the stones carefully to match the plants will greatly enhance the display. As the two groups have different growing cycles from most other succulents, they really need to be kept separate.

There is such a wide range of shapes, sizes, forms, textures and colours of succulent species that most people can usually find at least some plants amongst the various groups that appeal to them, which they would like to have growing as indoor plants.

Greenhouse cultivation

Succulents grow better in a greenhouse than indoors. The greenhouse will need to be kept frost-free in winter, preferably with a minimum temperature of at least 5°C (42°F), depending on the plants grown. Good air circulation is a great advantage and will help cut down damping-off and other problems in winter. During the summer good ventilation is essential as it is needed to cool the plants and stop them from scorching on the hottest days. Some of the more leafy succulents may require shade in the form of blinds or spray-on shading.

With more space available in a greenhouse than indoors, it is possible to grow a much wider, more diversified range of plants. In many of the more popular plant groups there are a vast number of different species and forms, and some collectors specialize in just one group. Since most collectors, however, find that their interests eventually change, a mixed collection might be more sensible for the collector starting out.

■ LEFT
Larger growing specimens are ideal for making a more permanent decorative feature in a conservatory.

When deciding what to grow, first see which plants are available in your area and then decide which most appeal to you. As a general rule, the more expensive the plant is, the rarer and probably more difficult it is to grow and keep in good condition. Check the more exotic plants' temperature requirements before you buy. If you cannot provide them easily, the plants will either suffer or more likely die.

You will also derive far more satisfaction from being able to grow your plants well, so that they look healthy, than from struggling with rare and unusual plants which often sulk because you cannot give them the exact conditions they require. This is often precisely why such plants are rare.

One of the more popular groups with collectors is the wide range of the Crassulaceae family, which includes many different genera. The most popular genera are *Crassula*, *Echeveria*, *Kalanchoe* and *Aeonium*. The other main group is the Aizoaceae family, which contains a very wide range of forms from large bushes (*Lampranthus*) to miniature, stone-like plants (*Lithops* and *Conophytum*).

■ ABOVE LEFT
The Crassulaceae family contains many diverse leafy succulents, most of which enjoy a bright position with some protection from the sun during fierce summer months.

■ LEFT
Those plants closely related to the *Aloe*, such as *Gasteria* and *Haworthia*, are easy to grow and attractive. Many are small growing and are ideal for windowsills and conservatories.

Outdoor cultivation

If you are fortunate enough to live in a mostly frost-free area, succulents can be grown outdoors. Some succulents can be seen growing on coastal rock faces in the warmer parts of the UK and USA and the big kinds of *Agave*, particularly the blue ones, will tolerate slight frosts, making them attractive feature plants for the garden. The shrubby Aizoaceae family will grow in very poor soil, the roots helping to stabilize fine or sandy ground.

The plants require good drainage and, depending on the winter temperatures, protection from the winter rains if in a cool area. Generally, plants seem able to tolerate temperatures a few degrees lower when outdoors, perhaps because of the better airflow. Local nurseries or garden centres will advise on plants suitable for the conditions in your area. Most succulents will not tolerate frost, and many – if they freeze – will collapse in a pile of mush.

However, in warm climates these plants are ideal for the garden since they tolerate low rainfall, and can more or less be left to their own devices once well established. This makes them perfect for landscaped gardens that are tended only occasionally. Many of the larger

and shrubby kinds of Aizoaceae make ideal bushes, producing their bright, daisy-like flowers at different times of the year. Among the *Agave*, larger *Aloe* and tall-growing *Euphorbia* are many wonderful plants which will add different shapes and textures. The small, brightly coloured rosettes of *Echeveria* also make excellent edging plants for beds. Larger-growing species, such as *Crassula ovata* and the penny plant (*Portulacaria afra*), can be used as hedging.

In colder climates, container plants can be placed outdoors

■ ABOVE
Broad, shallow containers can be planted with a mixture of succulents to decorate the garden during summer.

■ BELOW
This attractive, large, silver-blue, narrow-leafed species, *Agave americana*, is popular for outdoor landscaping. It is very robust and comparatively quick-growing, but take care – it can soon outgrow a small space.

■ LEFT
Plants such as *Echeveria* can be used as summer bedding plants or used in rockeries during the frost-free months.

If plants are being grown under protection during the winter, to be planted out during the summer, they will tend to have soft growth. These should be hardened off in spring in the shade, sheltered from strong winds for a couple of weeks, before being moved to their final positions.

■ ABOVE
Small, slow-growing succulents like *Sempervivum* can be used to fill small spaces in the garden.

in summer to decorate and add interest to the garden. Stable terracotta or heavy wooden containers are probably most suitable for this type of culture as the potting soil will dry more quickly after rain. Individual specimens of *Agave* make ideal spot plants and add interest to a patio or terrace. Other plants can either be grouped together, or larger specimens can be strategically placed to good effect amongst other plants.

The purple form of *Aeonium arborescens* makes taller, dark rosettes of feature plants in summer bedding. Many of the hardy *Sedum* and *Sempervivum* are ideal for rockeries, troughs or sink gardens. Smaller-growing plants can be planted in raised beds or troughs to create gardens in miniature. Interspersed with rocks of appropriate size and gravel, they create a pleasing, natural-looking arrangement.

Aeonium

These rosette succulents mostly come from the Canary Islands. They are quite diverse in habit, ranging from small, almost stemless rosettes to tall-stemmed plants, and from very small, bushy plants with minute rosettes to large, bushy ones. They are mostly winter-growing, and the flowers of most species appear in early spring or late winter. The growing point of the rosette turns into the flower stem which produces clusters of small, yellow, cream, pink, red or white flowers. Those listed require a minimum temperature of 5°C (42°F).

Because succulents are so diverse, it has been necessary to limit this section to cover only the more well-known species. An indication of size after five years' growth has been given for each of the species, though results can vary greatly, depending on cultivation. In fact, many of the more bushy species should be pruned occasionally rather than allowed to grow to their maximum size. A further selection of recommended succulents is given at the end of this book.

■ ABOVE

AEONIUM ARBOREUM

This tall species with shiny, green leaves is one of the most popular in this genus in cultivation, making a very attractive plant. Normally the heads will branch to form a cluster of 10cm (4in) rosettes. It requires a reasonable amount of water during spring and autumn, when most of its growth occurs. It will soon drop its leaves when too dry. Grown outdoors in summer, it makes an attractive bedding plant. The yellow flowers appear in spring. Five-years-old pot culture: height 1m (3ft); spread 60cm (2ft).

■ BELOW

*AEONIUM ARBOREUM
ATROPURPUREUM*

This attractive, purple-leafed form will
revert to green in winter, or if grown in
deep shade in summer. The darkest colour
is achieved in full sun. Because the leaves
are thin, scorching can occur in mid-
summer if the plants are too dry. As the
plants soon make new leaves, this is quickly
rectified. Ideal plants for summer planting
outdoors. Five-years-old pot culture:
height 1m (3ft); spread 60cm (2ft).

■ LEFT

*AEONIUM ARBOREUM
ALBOVARIEGATUM*

The green and cream of this variegated
form make it very popular. At the height
of summer the rosettes will sometimes turn
entirely cream, the green stripe reappearing
in the autumn. Five-years-old pot culture:
height 80cm (30in); spread 45cm (18in).

■ ABOVE

AEONIUM HAWORTHII

This bush-forming species produces blue-
green rosettes 5–8 cm (2–3in) in diameter
which are often edged with an eye-catching
red stripe in the summer. The clusters
of cream flowers appear in spring.
Five-years-old pot culture: height 30cm
(12in); spread 30cm (12in).

Agave

These new world plants come
from southern North America
and northern South America. The
virtually stemless rosettes vary greatly
in size, shape and colour, some being
almost hardy, others more tropical.
As a rough guide, the darker blue-
leafed species are much hardier than
those with pale green leaves. The
flowers are cream to white, often
completely without petals. After
flowering, most kinds of *Agave* will
slowly die, hopefully having made
some offsets. The following require a
minimum temperature of 5°C (42°F).

■ LEFT
AGAVE PARRYI

One of the most beautiful of the many
kinds of *Agave*, making medium-sized
rosettes of broad, grey-green leaves with
short, dark teeth. The plant is slow to
produce offsets and takes about 30 years
to reach maturity, flower and then die.
Five-years-old pot culture: height 15cm
(6in); spread 15cm (6in).

■ ABOVE
*AGAVE AMERICANA
MEDIOPICTA ALBA*

A striking blue-and-white-striped variety
which is much slower-growing and more
compact than the species. It is ideal for
growing in tubs or pots as a summer
garden feature. It is not as hardy as
the species. Five-years-old pot culture:
height 30cm (12in); spread 30cm (12in).

■ LEFT
AGAVE VICTORIA REGINAE

This slow-growing species takes about
35 years to reach flowering size. Small
plants have rosettes of outward-pointing
leaves, but after a number of years,
as the plant matures, the leaves become
incurving, giving the appearance of a large
football. Minimum temperature 5°C
(42°F). Five-years-old pot culture: height
10cm (4in); spread 15cm (6in).

Aloe

These plants are widespread from the African continent to the Middle East. There are many different species and forms, and it is often difficult to identify unusual plants with any degree of certainty. The different plants are quite varied in size, shape and colour. The smallest is no more than 2cm (¾in) in diameter, and the largest is nearly 10m (30ft) tall. Some rosettes are smooth, but many have small teeth along the edges of the leaves that make up the rosettes. Minimum temperature 7°C (45°F).

■ LEFT
ALOE RAMOSISSIMA

A large, bushy species, the stems dividing into two new heads at their tip. Comparatively slow-growing, taking many years to make a large plant, it is like a smaller version of *A. dichotoma*. Only very large plants will bear flowers. Five-years-old pot culture: height 10cm (4in); spread 5cm (2in).

■ BELOW
ALOE HUMILIS

A small, clumping species with stemless rosettes of blue leaves. The comparatively tall flowers are produced in early spring. Attractive, easy species to grow. Minimum temperature 5°C (42°F). Five-years-old pot culture: height 5cm (2in); spread 10cm (4in).

■ ABOVE
ALOE BARBADENSIS (SYN. *ALOE VERA*)

A plant well known for its medicinal properties as far back as the time of the pharaohs in ancient Egypt. A native of the Middle East, it has a number of forms, and the flowers can be either red or yellow. It is not particularly easy to grow, needing a minimum of about 10°C (50°F) in winter. It is quite prone to rotting if too wet. Five-years-old pot culture: height 30cm (12in); spread 10cm (4in).

Cheiridopsis

These clumping plants usually have swollen, blue leaves and are easy to flower in the spring or autumn. Many have small, blue, finger-like leaves, united at the base for some length with the upper part divided. Most are fairly easy to grow but will rot if grossly overwatered. Minimum temperature 3°C (37°F).

■ LEFT

CHEIRIDOPSIS PILLANSII (SYN. *C. CRASSA*)

This unusual species has very thick, swollen leaves, atypical of most of the others in this genus. Each successive pair of leaves are larger than the previous pair. The pale, daisy-like flowers appear only on larger specimens. Five-years-old pot culture: height 5cm (2in); spread 8cm (3in).

■ BELOW

CHEIRIDOPSIS VANZYLII

A small species that makes numerous heads in a small clump. Flowers in spring or autumn. Five-years-old pot culture: height 5cm (2in); spread 8cm (3in).

■ LEFT

CHEIRIDOPSIS DENTICULATA

More typical of most of the plants in the genus in leaf shape, although size can vary a great deal. Clumps with age to make a very attractive specimen. Spring flowering. Five-years-old pot culture: height 8cm (3in); spread 8cm (3in).

Conophytum

The mainly very small, clumping
plants of this genus are rather like
peas. Some species, like *C. bilobum*,
have two 'ears'; others, such as *C.
calculus*, have flattened tops; and the
majority have small, rounded bodies,
made up of two united stem-like
leaves, with a small fissure between
them. The flowers normally appear in
autumn. Although there are exceptions,
most of the bilobed species have
yellow flowers, and most of the pea-
like ones have pink or occasionally
yellow flowers. There are also a few
night-flowering species which tend to
be scented, with very narrow petals.
Minimum temperature 4°C (39°F).

■ BELOW
CONOPHYTUM CALCULUS

The slightly larger, pale green bodies of
this species make it quite distinctive. The
nocturnal yellow to orange flowers are
clove-scented. Five-years-old pot culture:
height 1cm (½in); spread 3cm (1in).

■ ABOVE
CONOPHYTUM BILOBUM

This species now embodies a large number of the old 'species'
with two 'ears'. The plants under this name are extremely variable
in size and shape, although all have the two 'ears'. Yellow flowers.
Five-years-old pot culture: height 3cm (1in); spread 3cm (1in).

CONOPHYTUM TAYLORIANUM
V. ERNIANUM

The pale grey-green colour of the short, squat plant bodies and the often pinched shape of the two 'ears' make this a distinctive species. The flowers are pink to carmine. Five-years-old pot culture: height 3cm (1in); spread 3cm (1in).

■ BELOW

CONOPHYTUM WETTSTEINII

The broad, flat, pale heads of this species with just a central fissure are the distinguishing features. Although the fissure can vary in size and shape, it is quite distinctive. The flowers are mostly pink, or occasionally whitish. Five-years-old pot culture: height 1cm (½in); spread 3cm (1in).

■ ABOVE

CONOPHYTUM UVIFORME (SLEEPING)

In late spring, the plants will shrivel almost overnight within their papery skins, and rest through the summer until the cooler weather of early autumn. During this time, when they are described as 'sleeping', they require occasional light watering. When the temperatures begin to lower in early autumn, the plants need two or three good soakings to break their dormancy.

Cotyledon

A group of mostly bushy succulents producing relatively large, bell-shaped flowers that range in colour from red or pink to pale yellow. Slow- to moderately fast-growing, this large genus of plants varies from small, shrubby species to large, much bushier plants. The leaf shape, colour, size and texture are all quite variable. Minimum temperature 7°C (45°F).

■ ABOVE
COTYLEDON UNDULATA

Although attractive as a small plant, this will grow up to 60cm (2ft) high, and make an eye-catching bush. The large, rounded, grey, powdery leaves are often flat at the top, and the margin undulates like a concertina. If the plant is grown outdoors, where the ultra-violet light is not filtered by glass, the leaves turn a deep reddish-purple under their powdery, white farina. The orange to red flowers appear in late summer. Five-years-old pot culture: height 25cm (10in); spread 15cm (6in).

■ LEFT
COTYLEDON WOODII

A small, bushy species with small, nearly circular, dark green leaves, sometimes covered with a slight, white, waxy coating. The relatively large, dark red, bell-shaped flowers appear in autumn. Five-years-old pot culture: height 25cm (10in); spread 25cm (10in).

Crassula

This group contains a diverse number of plants producing clusters of small flowers. The plants range from the very small and compact to the large and tree-like. Most species have thickened, fleshy leaves, some minute, others quite large. The leaf texture varies: some are shiny and glossy, others rough and waxy. The leaf colour ranges from bright, glossy green to grey and white in many small species. Minimum temperature 5°C (42°F).

■ ABOVE

CRASSULA MESEMBRYANTHOIDES

A bushy species with tiny, sausage-shaped leaves covered in short hairs. The small, yellowish flowers appear in late summer. Five-years-old pot culture: height 30cm (12in); spread 40cm (15in).

■ ABOVE

CRASSULA OVATA

The money plant is probably the most widely grown member of this genus, and is popular as a bonsai plant. It will survive quite well under adverse conditions, but if given full sun in summer, and fed and watered well, it bears small, white flowers in autumn on larger plants. They last for several weeks if the plant is not kept too warm. Minimum temperature 3°C (37°F), but 7°C (45°F) is better. Five-years-old pot culture: height 45cm (18in); spread 30cm (12in).

■ LEFT

CRASSULA 'MORGAN'S PINK'

This charming hybrid is magnificent in late winter when it comes into flower with its delicate cluster of small, pink blooms. The plant soon makes offsets of almost stemless clumps close to the ground and, although slow-growing, the clumps will soon reach 12–15cm (5–6in) in diameter. Larger plants tend to be much more prone to rot as there is little air circulation between the close-packed leaves to dry any surplus moisture or condensation. Minimum temperature 10°C (50°F). Five-years-old pot culture: height 10cm (4in); spread 16cm (7in).

Dudleya

These rosette plants are closely related to the *Echeveria,* but are usually white to silver in colour, mainly covered in a powdery, white farina. Minimum temperature 3°C (37°F).

■ BELOW
DUDLEYA BRITTONII

Perhaps the most beautiful of this genus, with rosettes of broad, white, powdery leaves. This species is slow to branch, and will normally do so only on old plants with longish stems. Reasonably easy to grow, it requires full sun for the best colour. It is advisable not to handle the plants too much, as the white, waxy farina on the leaves is easily removed. Minimum temperature 3°C (37°F). Five-years-old pot culture: height 10cm (4in); spread 10cm (4in).

■ ABOVE
DUDLEYA HASSEI

This bushy species offsets freely to make broad, short clumps. The silvery leaves are almost cylindrical in shape. Minimum temperature 3°C (37°F). Five-years-old pot culture: height 12cm (5in); spread 30cm (12in).

Echeveria

A large group of rosette plants, many almost stemless, amd others bushy or on tall stems. The rosettes are of mostly broad leaves often coloured blue, red or purple. The flowers appear on tall spikes and are bell-shaped, often orange-red, occasionally yellow. Some species are summer-flowering, others produce their flowers from autumn to winter. The plants hybridize easily with many of the other similar groups in the Crassulaceae family. This makes the identification of unnamed plants extremely difficult, more so as many change their form slightly, depending on growing conditions. Those listed here require a minimum temperature of 5°C (42°F).

■ ABOVE
ECHEVERIA 'FROSTY'

This small, bushy species has rosettes of silvery-blue leaves which are covered in short hairs. The plants eventually become quite bushy, producing their spikes of orange flowers during the summer and autumn. Five-years-old pot culture: height 30cm (12in); spread 40cm (15in).

■ LEFT
ECHEVERIA AGAVOIDES

The large rosettes of this broad, pointed-leafed species are a pale olive green, sometimes tinged red, sometimes with a roughened texture. It is quite distinctive in appearance, but has small, uninteresting flowers. Five-years-old pot culture: height 8cm (3in); spread 12cm (5in).

Euphorbia

Most major land masses throughout the world have their own indigenous species of *Euphorbia*. The habitats range from arctic tundra to tropical rock pools. With a large group like this it is often very difficult to decide which species are succulent and which are not. There are reputedly over 1,200 succulent species, those that are normally collected coming from frost-free areas. They are completely diverse in character, ranging from leafy bushes to highly succulent, cactus-like shapes. Most are susceptible to low temperatures, and the more tropical species need in excess of 10°C (50°F) in winter.

■ ABOVE
EUPHORBIA MILII

This bushy species from Madagascar is well known as a house plant. It needs a minimum temperature of about 16°C (60°F) to grow really well, making it more suitable for indoor than glasshouse culture, and it should flower through most of the year. When in growth it needs a moderate amount of water, but if kept at lower temperatures water should be withheld. Five-years-old pot culture: height 60cm (2ft); spread 30cm (1ft).

■ ABOVE
EUPHORBIA HORRIDA

This cactus-like species is quite variable in diameter and colour; the short, swollen, ribbed stems range from a grey-white green to almost green. It is a very attractive, slow-growing species, but needs at least 7°C (45°F) in winter when kept completely dry. Five-years-old pot culture: height 7cm (3in); spread 3cm (1in).

■ LEFT
EUPHORBIA OBESA CRISTATE

A small, globular species eventually becoming a short column. The almost hemispherical body has a number of poorly defined ribs and the plant is covered in banded markings like chevrons, giving rise to one of its common names, the tartan golf ball. Keep completely dry in winter as it is prone to rotting at lower temperatures. Minimum temperature 10°C (50°F). Five-years-old pot culture: height 5cm (2in); spread 7cm (3in).

Faucaria

Gasteria

Quite a number of *Gasteria* produce a fan of leaves when young, but they mostly become a rosette on older plants. The flowers are usually green, red and yellow. Related to the *Aloe*, *Gasteria* also have long-lasting, tubular to bell-shaped flowers that are swollen in the middle like a stomach; it is these that give the plant its name. Minimum temperature 2°C (35°F).

■ BELOW
GASTERIA NITIDA

This very large form or hybrid is quite unusual. Unlike many in this species, it is very slow to offset. The flowers are produced in mid-summer. Five-years-old pot culture: height 10cm (4in); spread 10cm (4in).

These small, clumping plants have short, thick, chunky leaves with teeth-like growths along their margins. Most of their growth is from mid-summer until late autumn, when they produce bright yellow, daisy-like flowers. Minimum temperature 5°C (42°F).

■ ABOVE
FAUCARIA TIGRINA

This species is perhaps the most common, although the others are very similar. The golden flowers are produced in autumn. Five-years-old pot culture: height 7cm (3in); spread 12cm (5in).

Haworthia

A medium-sized group of small, stemless, rosette-forming plants, quite diverse in leaf shape and colour, mostly clumping, a few becoming columnar with tightly packed leaves. The plants are mostly free-flowering, producing their long, slender flower spikes over a long period from spring to autumn. The small, white flowers are well spaced along the stem. Minimum temperature 3°C (37°F).

■ ABOVE

HAWORTHIA COOPERI

The rosettes of this species have thick, globular, fleshy leaves which are translucent at their tips. It prefers shade in summer or the leaf tips will shrivel, although new leaves in autumn soon replace them. Five-years-old pot culture: height 5cm (2in); spread 7cm (3in).

■ LEFT

HAWORTHIA VENOSA V. TESSELATA

The small rosettes of this species are composed of a few thick, chunky, angular leaves. The upper surface is usually well marked with translucent lines. The plants offset freely by underground stolons, soon making fine colonies. There are many different forms, both in size and leaf markings. Five-years-old pot culture: height 5cm (2in); spread 12cm (5in).

■ RIGHT

HAWORTHIA ATTENUATA

Widely distributed in cultivation, it is often wrongly labelled as *H. fasciata* which, while similar, is a larger plant, fairly rare in cultivation. This species is easy to grow, occasionally tolerating temperatures near freezing. Grown in full sun, with little water, the plant will rest in summer when the green leaves will turn reddish. Grown in the shade with more water, it will stay green and grow quickly. The green leaves are marked with raised white dots which vary even between individual plants. It is difficult to find two exactly matching plants, unless they both have the same parent. Five-years-old pot culture: height 5cm (2in); spread 7cm (3in).

Hoya

Kalanchoe

These mostly climbing plants prefer shade; many come from tropical jungles. They are naturally widespread in the world and are found in a wide range of differing climates. Although a few are bushy, most have long, slender stems which produce opposite leaves, usually with a long internodal gap. The clusters of small, wax-like flowers appear in summer and autumn. Some are easy to grow, others extremely difficult. Minimum temperature 7–21°C (45–70°F).

A medium-sized group of mostly shrubby or trailing plants ranging from small to almost tree-like. *Kalanchoe* may be grouped with *Bryophyllum*, plants with fleshy leaves that make plantlets from their edges. Many species require a number of short days to initiate flowering, and so are naturally spring-flowering. Some commercial species, such as 'Flaming Katy', can be made to flower at any time of year by manipulating the day length. Most are easy to grow, but some species require 10°C (50°F) in winter.

■ ABOVE
KALANCHOE BEHARENSIS

The large, velvety leaves of this species make it distinctive. A large plant, it makes a small tree or bush in time. The small terminal flowers on larger plants are cup-shaped and brownish-yellow. As this plant comes from Madagascar, it is sensitive to cold and should be kept above 10°C (50°F) in winter. Five-years-old pot culture: height 1m (3ft); spread 20cm (8in).

■ ABOVE
HOYA IMPERIALIS

For many collectors of this group, *H. imperialis* is the species to acquire. It is very difficult to find and expensive to buy. It has large, red flowers and is extremely difficult to grow, seeming to require a temperature of about 21°C (70°F). One for the specialist. Five-years-old pot culture: height 3m (9ft); spread climbing.

■ LEFT
KALANCHOE
DAIGREMONTIANA HYBRID

This is one of the plants sometimes called *Bryophyllum*, the group of *Kalanchoe* that produces new plantlets freely from the leaf margins. The plants are easy to grow and the detached offsets will grow almost anywhere, even on the curtains and in the carpet. Grown well in pots, and cared for, the plants will produce their orange, bell-shaped flowers on tall stems in early spring. Minimum temperature 2°C (35°F). Five-years-old pot culture: height 1m (3ft); spread 60cm (2ft).

Kleinia

The genera of *Senecio* and *Kleinia* were confused, and some years ago were united into one group, *Senecio*. More recently the group has been divided again, and *Senecio* now contains those species with the larger yellow flowers, while *Kleinia* embodies those with small 'flowers' lacking the ray florets. These flowers are really composed of many very small, individual flowers enclosed in a small, cylindrical sheath. Minimum temperature 7°C (45°F).

■ ABOVE
KLEINIA NERIFOLIA (SYN. *SENECIO KLEINIA*)

This large-growing bushy species from the Canary Islands is rather attractive as a small specimen, reminiscent of a small, grey-green-stemmed palm tree. During the winter, with the poor light in northern latitudes, water should be applied very sparingly to stop the plant becoming etiolated. Cuttings should be taken in mid-summer, dried until calloused and rooted in autumn, when the main plant starts growing. Five-years-old pot culture: height 1.6m (5ft); spread 60cm (2ft).

Lampranthus

A large group of shrubby or bushy plants from the Aizoaceae family. Most are cultivated for their flowers: they make magnificent spreads of colour when grown permanently outdoors in frost-free areas. Eventually they become very woody and can die. It is therefore worth propagating new plants every three to four years from cuttings. These plants must have full sun for their flowers to open fully. Minimum temperature 1°C (34°F).

■ BELOW
LAMPRANTHUS HAWORTHII

Of all the succulent plants, this must be the most spectacular when in flower. In spring it is completely covered in deep pink flowers, 5–8cm (2–3in) wide, which are delicately perfumed. It will soon become quite a large bush; small plants can be pruned after flowering to keep a neat shape, and larger plants can be trimmed and made into a short, box-like hedge. Five-years-old pot culture: height 60cm (2ft); spread 1m (3ft).

Lithops

This charming group of stone-like plants contains over 100 different species and forms. Each plant is composed of a pair of swollen, united leaves with a small fissure across the centre of each head. Plants are mostly bluish-grey to brown, with just a few green species. Extremely sensitive to overwatering; during winter they should be kept completely dry. Minimum temperature 1°C (34°F), though 7°C (45°F) is safer.

■ BELOW
LITHOPS AUCAMPIAE

This chocolate-brown species is one of the larger-growing ones, with individual heads up to 5–8cm (2–3in) long. The upper surface of the leaves is usually flat. Five-years-old pot culture: height 3cm (1in); spread 3cm (1in).

■ BELOW
LITHOPS LESLIEI

The largest-growing *Lithops*, very similar to *L. aucampiae*, but the upper surface of the leaves is usually slightly domed. Five-years-old pot culture: height 3cm (1in); spread 3cm (1in).

■ ABOVE
LITHOPS KARASMONTANA
(F. MICKBERGENSIS)

A variable species, the flat-topped crescent-shaped leaves are shades of grey to brown. Five-years-old pot culture: height 3cm (1in); spread 3cm (1in).

■ ABOVE
LITHOPS
PSEUDOTRUNCATELLA

Seedlings of this species are distinctive, as the fissure between the leaves is like a small slot. When the plants are mature, they usually turn grey, but sometimes they have brownish markings on their often unequal-sized leaves. These plants are normally one of the first to come into flower in late summer. Five-years-old pot culture: height 3cm (1in); spread 3cm (1in).

Pachypodium

This genus is closely related to *Adenium*, but has 'spines'. The plants mostly have swollen stems, often thick and chunky, producing more slender branches. The caudex is often partly buried. Most are tricky to grow, some very difficult. The easiest are the southern African species; the most difficult from the hot, dry parts of northern Africa and Madagascar. Minimum temperature 10–15°C (50–60°F).

■ BELOW
PACHYPODIUM BISPINOSUM

This South African species makes a large, swollen base, narrowing above ground to produce more slender, arching branches. The flowers appear repeatedly through the summer. It can survive the occasional low temperature but prefers 7°C (45°F) in winter. It requires moderate watering in summer. Five-years-old pot culture: height 15cm (6in); spread 5cm (2in).

■ ABOVE
PACHYPODIUM GEAYI

P. lamerei and *P. geayi* are different from most of the other members of this genus, as they are tall-growing, tree-like species. Provide warm conditions and frequent watering in summer, but not a wet and soggy potting soil. Plants will flower when 1.2–2m (4–6ft). After flowering, the stems branch to make a tree-like shape. Minimum temperature 15°C (60°F). Five-years-old pot culture: height 30cm (12in); spread 12cm (5in).

Pelargonium

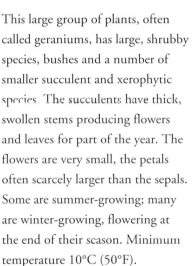

This large group of plants, often called geraniums, has large, shrubby species, bushes and a number of smaller succulent and xerophytic species. The succulents have thick, swollen stems producing flowers and leaves for part of the year. The flowers are very small, the petals often scarcely larger than the sepals. Some are summer-growing; many are winter-growing, flowering at the end of their season. Minimum temperature 10°C (50°F).

■ ABOVE
PELARGONIUM ALTERNANS

This interesting, semi-succulent species has swollen, stick-like stems and tends to be dormant in summer. It comes back into full growth during the autumn–spring period, although it can produce flowers throughout the year. Avoid overwatering at any time, giving small amounts occasionally when the plant is semi-dormant. Minimum temperature 7°C (45°F). Five-years-old pot culture: height 15cm (6in); spread 15cm (6in).

Pleiospilos

Portulacaria

This bush-like species has graceful, arching branches and small, roundish leaves when the plants are small. It makes an attractive pot plant or bonsai, particularly the variegated form. In frost-free areas it is sometimes used for hedging as large, mature specimens produce much more erect, thicker and stronger stems. Seldom flowers in cultivation. Minimum temperature 7°C (45°F).

■ BELOW
PORTULACARIA AFRA

The arching stems of this species make it useful for indoor culture as a house plant. Prune frequently to keep a good shape. Five-years-old pot culture: height 30cm (12in); spread 30cm (12in).

Commonly called living granite, due to the mostly thickened, grey leaves resembling pieces of granite. They produce large, yellow flowers, sometimes coconut-scented, in autumn. They are easy to grow, though plants can be quite prone to red spider mite. Minimum temperature 5°C (42°F).

■ ABOVE
PLEIOSPILOS COMPACTUS

Until fairly recently there were many names in this genus for plants that appeared similar. Those species with thick, pointed leaves have now mostly been amalgamated under *P. compactus*, excluding those with rounded ends to the leaves. The plants make small clumps with 2–6 leaves per head. The 5–7cm (2–3in) yellow flowers appear in autumn. Indented brown markings on the leaves are often the sign of red spider mite damage, to which the plants are prone. Easy to grow and flower. Five-years-old pot culture: height 7cm (3in); spread 12cm (5in).

Sedum

A group of plants well distributed throughout the world, some hardy, some quite tropical. This large group has recently been split into many new genera, many of the old sections now genera in their own right. In practice, however, many of the old names are still used. The plants can be ground cover, bushes, shrubs or almost tree-like. The hardy species are well known and make good rockery plants. Many of the tender species are ideal for hanging baskets. Minimum temperature 10°C (50°F), though varies among the species.

■ ABOVE

*SEDUM RUBROTINCTUM
AURORA*

Far prettier than the species, this form has pink to yellow leaves that become more intense if it is grown in full sun. Propagate from rosettes; if leaves are used the colour reverts to green. Minimum temperature 1°C (34°F). Five-years-old pot culture: height 20cm (8in); spread 1m (3ft).

Testudinaria

This small, fascinating group of plants has thickened, swollen bases or tubers which can grow to 1m (3ft) across and produce slender annual vines with thin, heart-shaped leaves. The small, yellowish-green flowers are unisexual and inconspicuous, being produced towards the tips of the climbing stems. Most species are similar; some produce an above-ground caudex, others are subterranean and are sometimes called *Dioscorea*. Water plants moderately in the growing season. Minimum temperature 10°C (50°F).

■ LEFT

*TESTUDINARIA
ELEPHANTIPES*

This is probably the best-known and most widely cultivated species in the genus. It is winter-growing and produces a 1m (3ft) hemispherical caudex which is deeply fissured, giving the appearance of being carved in cork. Plants normally start into growth in late summer and return to dormancy in spring, resting through the summer. In the early part of the growing season the plants require moderate amounts of water to break dormancy, tailing off as winter progresses. Plant with the base below the soil to avoid dehydration. Light watering should be given during summer to prevent desiccation. Five-years-old pot culture: height (caudex) 5cm (2in); spread 7cm (3in).

Care and cultivation

■ ABOVE
When the weather is warm, watering from above will wash the plants clean and remove any dusty deposits.

■ OPPOSITE
The tall swollen trunks of the pony tail palm (*Nolina recurvata*) branch easily when cut or damaged in the crown.

Whether succulents are to be grown indoors or outside, their requirements are much the same. They need an open, free-draining potting soil mix containing about one-third sharp, small grit, the rest being peat, loam or another potting soil mix, complete with a good base fertilizer. Succulents are hungry plants, and many come from areas which, while low in humus, are rich in mineral content. For the best results, both in growth and flowers, fertilize the plants regularly about once a week during the growing season (mostly from spring until autumn) with a cactus fertilizer or one recommended for tomatoes at about half-strength.

Stem succulents

The stem succulents are usually quite diverse in their requirements. The majority of succulents in cultivation come from the old world, with the exception of the *Agave* and *Echeveria*. In Africa, they can be found from Saudi Arabia to South Africa. Needless to say, that covers almost every likely habitat for succulents.

Many succulents, particularly in the genus *Euphorbia*, have, through evolution, adapted to shapes very similar to those of the cacti found in the Americas, which cover similar latitudes. Most of the succulent *Euphorbias* do not really like temperatures below 10°C (50°F), some of those from Madagascar and North Africa needing a minimum of 15°C (60°F). Most are quite prone to rotting at low temperatures, especially if kept too wet. Some of the larger, tree-like species are more tolerant of slightly adverse conditions, when well established.

The *Tylecodon* (the stem succulent *Cotyledon*) and the *Cyphostemma* (the caudex-forming *Cissus*) are two other groups of larger-growing southern African stem succulents. Neither is particularly easy to grow, especially the first, which is winter-growing.

One quite large group of small-growing, stem succulents are the Stapeliads. There are over 700 species in many different genera. Most are like clusters of short, green fingers with star-shaped flowers. There have been many name changes in the group lately, but they have not generally met with much approval. Apart from a few common species, they can be as challenging to grow as any succulents. They are probably one of the most difficult groups to grow well in Europe.

A few American stem succulents are well known in cultivation, such as the pony tail palm (*Nolina recurvata*) and boojum (*Fouquieria* [*Idria*] *columnaris*). The *Burseras* (Burseraceae family) make fine bushes, growing in summer but normally deciduous in winter. They need moderate watering when growing, being almost dry while at rest.

Bushy leaf succulents

This group is one of the largest, covering all those plants with thickened, fleshy leaves, but otherwise looking more like normal plants. In this group, Crassulaceae is probably the largest family, covering *Crassula*, *Kalanchoe*, *Cotyledon*, *Adromischus* and *Sedum*. Aizoaceae is another large group with bushy kinds, such as *Lampranthus*, *Delosperma* and *Drosanthemum*. Many other genera also contain some species that are bush-like.

Most of this group are generally easy to grow, many growing throughout the year if conditions are favourable. Although some plants need higher temperatures, most will survive at about 7°C (45°F). It may be necessary to give these plants small amounts of water occasionally during winter to prevent undue shrivelling or leaf drop. At lower temperatures, however, with a high humidity, plants can be quite prone to rotting. It is therefore advisable to keep the temperature at 7°C (45°F) minimum, and to provide good air movement by using a fan or fan heater. Most of these plants will dramatically collapse immediately if frozen, even for a short period.

Highly succulent-leafed succulents

Most of the plants with highly
succulent, swollen leaves tend to be a
little slower-growing. Because of their
normally low habit and ability to
store water, they are usually far more
prone to rotting if overwatered. One
of the most highly developed in this
group are the *Lithops,* with a body
composed of one swollen, united
pair of leaves.

A large number of plants in
this group are to be found in the
Aizoaceae family, ranging from very
small, pea-like bodies (*Conophytum*)
to large, fat, finger-like leaves
(*Glottiphyllum*). Many of these plants
have a fairly short growing season,
requiring comparatively little
water during the rest of the year.
Surprisingly, many of the plants in
this group can tolerate quite low
temperatures: 2–3°C (35–37°F)
if completely dry.

Some of the Crassulaceae family
make tight rosettes of swollen leaves,
as in the case of many *Echeveria* and
Sempervivum, both of which can
tolerate long periods of drought.
They are mostly quite easy to grow,
and the hardy kinds of *Sempervivum*
make good rockery plants. The
different *Echeveria* are often used by
parks departments in summer for
outdoor bedding schemes.

Choosing your plants

Succulents can be purchased
from a variety of sources, including
florists, supermarkets and garden
centres. Sometimes, though, the
plants are not kept in peak condition.
At worst, they might be covered in
insect pests, particularly mealy bug,
and almost be falling out of their
pots, suffering from dehydration.
Such plants do little to encourage
the new collector.

Your chosen plants should look
in peak condition, glowing with
good health. The leaves should be
complete, not broken, and the stems
should be erect – except in the case of
a pendent or creeping plant. Good
colour is vital, so avoid the pale and
anaemic. Ideally, plants should also
be named correctly, but labels do fall
out, and people reading them can put
them back in the wrong place. This is
an occupational hazard.

If you are at all doubtful about the
health of a plant, try repotting it.
With a little effort and patience, you
may well find that it grows into an
impressive specimen.

Planting succulents

Growing several plants together in one container is a good way of making an attractive display with a few plants. When choosing a suitable container, remember that the plants need a bright situation. Make sure that the container is not too large or the wrong shape for its intended position. Containers can be plastic, terracotta or ceramic, and some of the larger bonsai bowls can be used to good effect. A container with drainage holes is easier to look after.

Growing succulents in containers

For a bowl garden, choose plants that require similar growing conditions. Try to select plants that are not fast-growing, so that the arrangement will not overgrow too quickly. Also choose plants that require similar amounts of water at the same time of year, and pick a variety of different shapes, colours and textures that will enhance the overall display.

During the summer, a regular watering every two or three weeks should suffice. Containers without drainage holes need to be watered carefully so as not to build up a reservoir at their base. Ideally, enough water should be given at

a time so that the soil will dry out in 10 days. Feed occasionally to keep the plants healthy, but not to make them grow too quickly and become overcrowded. Should one or two branches of any plant grow too long, trim them back with scissors or secateurs (pruners) in warm weather.

PLANTING A SUCCULENT BOWL GARDEN

1 Begin by placing the plants in the container, and arrange them for the best effect. Do not overcrowd the plants – this will detract from the overall look.

2 Next, fill the container with potting soil and carefully plant the specimens, firming well; it is surprising how much it will settle.

3 Decorate the top of the container with some pieces of rock, and top-dress with small gravel. A small paintbrush is very useful for dusting the rocks and pushing the gravel under the plants.

4 When it is finished, stand back and take a look. If any changes need to be made, do them now before the root systems get tangled up. Water very lightly overhead with a rose or spray to settle the gravel.

Building a raised bed

Succulents can be grown outdoors in a frost-free area. The plants need a well-drained soil which can be achieved by mixing about equal proportions of potting soil and grit. If the bed is raised above ground level, it is easier for the surplus water to drain away. If there is high rainfall, particularly in winter, the plants will need some form of protection.

In areas that are likely to have frosts, it is better to construct a bed in a greenhouse or conservatory. The bed needs a depth of 10–30cm (4–12in) of potting soil depending on the size of plants to be grown. Permanent beds can be built with brick or stone.

Line the bottom and any exterior walls with polystyrene (Styrofoam) to stop the cold penetrating the bed and damaging the plants. Fill to within 10–30cm (4 –12in) of the top with rubble (hardcore), and then cover with a permeable membrane, such as carpet, underfelt or even newspaper, to stop the potting soil sinking into the rubble. Next, top up the bed with a gritty potting soil containing at least one third gravel, then firm the bed well to reduce subsequent settlement.

PLANTING A PERMANENT RAISED BED

1 A raised bed should consist of the following: hardcore to allow free drainage; a membrane to stop any soil from filtering into the hardcore; a layer of gritty soil; and a top layer of gravel.

2 Having decided upon a location, arrange the plants for best effect, digging out suitable holes to plant them.

3 When you remove the plants from their pots, carefully open up any tight, downward spiral of roots before planting. Gently firm them into place.

4 After planting, top-dress with gravel. Avoid artificially coloured gravels – pieces of rock placed between the plants will create a more natural-looking effect. It is best to allow the bed to settle for a week or so before watering properly.

Using hanging baskets

Many of the small, shrubby succulents are perfect for hanging baskets as they soon overflow from small pots and hang down the sides. Some of the best plants to choose are members of the Crassulaceae family. Apart from the larger, bush-forming species, many kinds of *Crassula* and *Kalanchoe* make ideal subjects cascading over the edges of the pots. Good examples are the smaller *Kalanchoe* such as *K. pumila*, *K.* 'Tessa' and *K.* 'Wendy', and most of the small-growing *Crassula* species. Individual members of some of the other groups, such as the heart vine (*Ceropegia woodii*) and *Senecio* (*Kleinia*) *rowleyanus,* are always popular as house plants. In very bright situations, a number of the shrubby kinds of Aizoaceae family, such as *Lampranthus, Delosperma* and *Oscularia*, also make fine specimens.

Select a basket to suit the location. There is a wide selection of metal, plastic and wire ones readily available from gardening outlets. Wire baskets will require a liner before they arc filled with potting soil. If space is at a premium, several different species of succulent can be planted in the same container, although one or two are sure to outgrow the others. Planting two or three smaller plants of the same species in a basket will rapidly make a more natural-looking display.

Some of the more shrubby succulents will need protection from direct sun in summer. Hanging pots and baskets dry out much more quickly than those at ground level. In summer, they should be watered well and then allowed to dry before they are watered again; in winter, they should be given only enough water to prevent the plants from shrivelling. Larger containers can be very slow to dry in cool weather.

PLANTING A HANGING BASKET

1 Assemble a selection of plants and some free-draining potting soil. Make sure that the plants are not obstructed by the hanging chains.

2 Arrange the plants around the edge of the bowl, leaning them slightly outwards to encourage the growth to become pendent.

3 When they are all planted, firm the potting soil well, leaving a 3cm (1in) gap at the top of the pot to allow for watering.

Routine maintenance

Some succulents will tolerate a great deal of neglect, and even after a prolonged drought, will soon revive with a drink of water. However, they are more likely to thrive if treated with care, based on a knowledge of their requirements.

Dust

Plants grown indoors tend to accumulate dust. Remove with a small brush, blow off with a hair dryer, or wash off with a water spray. In a greenhouse, overhead watering will normally remove a build-up of dust.

Handling

Some succulents, such as the *Euphorbia*, *Agave* and *Aloe*, are thorny plants, and there are many methods for handling them. A pair of domestic rubber gloves or a paper collar give fairly good protection for smaller plants. With larger specimens, one or two cloths give good protection.

Euphorbia is one of the worst groups to handle, for the plants exude a sticky and corrosive latex. On soft or tender skin it can cause burning, but it can be washed off with paraffin (glycerine soap) or turpentine – water can set the latex, and the resulting rubbery solution sticks resolutely to the skin. A pair of domestic rubber gloves gives good protection when handling these plants.

Damaged plants

Although the leafy succulent plants keep their leaves for a long time, they eventually shed their older leaves. Dead leaves should be removed, as they make an ideal nest for pests. Sometimes branches may die back from the tips or be broken off, and they can be removed with a pair of

PRUNING SUCCULENTS

1 Some of the very succulent-leafed plants such as *Lithops* and *Conophytum* absorb nutrients and moisture from the old leaves into the new ones, leaving behind papery shells. These can be removed with a pair of tweezers, but care is needed not to pull off the new heads, as they have very thin stems.

2 Most bushy or shrubby plants produce their shoots in what appears to be a haphazard fashion, influenced by many external forces. Some shoots will grow long and leggy, and some in the wrong place. Both must be shortened from time to time to keep the plants in good shape.

3 After being pruned, most succulents will shoot out again from the point where they were cut or just below, often making several stems where there was one, as can be seen in this *Crassula ovata*.

secateurs (pruners). You must also remove dead flowers and, after the last has faded, the entire flower stem, snipping it off at the base.

Note too that clump-forming plants sometimes force off their offsets, and unless they are removed and planted, they will die. The heads in a clump that are discoloured or look shrivelled can often be pulled out, but sometimes a small, sharp knife must be inserted between the heads to sever them at their base.

Finally, plants should be regularly inspected for rot or signs of fungal growth during damp and cool weather. Any infected leaves should be removed immediately to prevent further spread of the disease. Large, freshly cut areas can be treated with a fungicide, such as green sulphur.

Pruning

Most of the cultivated succulents are perennial, and many are bushes, trees or carpeting plants where they grow naturally. Some species are used for hedging, others for stabilizing and binding poor soils. Many of the larger-growing specimens will eventually make fine trees.

If you live in an area where succulents can be grown outdoors as garden plants and space is not a problem, you can leave them to grow unchecked. Unfortunately, as most of us have to protect these plants during parts of the year and space is at a premium, most will ultimately need to be pruned. It is a good idea to prune and tidy plants just before repotting them. When pruning, cut back far enough to allow for a reasonable period of further growth.

Watering and feeding

Like all plants, succulents must have food, water, light and air to grow. During the spring to autumn period, most succulents should be watered well and then left to dry out before watering again. Weather, situation, soil, temperature, pot size and type of plant will all affect how quickly or slowly this happens. Ideally, with larger containers, sufficient water should be given at a time so that the containers will dry out in about 10 days. Smaller pots, even when watered well, may dry out in three days in hot weather.

If you grow all your plants in a similar potting soil, it makes it easier to judge how often to water. Succulents seem to be quite hungry plants, and a regular dose of low-nitrogen cactus fertilizer added to the water will greatly improve the plants. There is no need, however, to feed more often than once a week.

PRUNING BACK DEAD AND OLD LEAVES AND STEMS

1 Dead flower stems can easily be removed with secateurs (pruners) or scissors, shown here with *Echeveria.*

2 After removing the dead leaves from an old *Echeveria,* old portions of stem can be cut away and the plant repotted.

Repotting

Succulents need repotting from time to time, and should look comfortable in their pots. How often this is done depends mainly on the plant's growth rate. With most of the small plants it is time to repot when the plants so thicken that they almost reach the sides of the container. The new pot should allow for a 3cm (1in) space between the plant and the side of the pot. Larger plants require a little more space, perhaps 3–5cm (1–2in). Many of the low-growing, spreading succulents will probably do best in

shallow pans. The best guide really is visual – does the plant look right in the pot? Tall-growing plants need a pot in proportion to their height. If the plant is top-heavy or unstable, the pot is certainly too small. A bushy plant 60cm (2ft) tall will need at least a 20cm (8in) pot, if not larger.

After the plant has been in a pot for two to three years the potting soil will have become compacted, and both air and water will have difficulty getting to the roots. In hard-water areas, the level of chalk (lime) will

also have increased, together with any unused compounds from feeding. Most succulents will therefore benefit from repotting from time to time, even if only to freshen the potting soil and keep the plants healthy. Preferably repot small plants every two to three years, large ones every four years. Spring, or the start of the growing season in the case of winter growers, is the ideal time. If, however, your plant is desperate, it is better to repot it at any time of year rather than wait six months.

TIPS FOR REPOTTING SUCCULENTS

1 To repot a succulent, you will need a new pot, enough semi-dry potting soil to fill it and, if the plant is thorny, something to hold it. A collar of paper is ideal for thorny plants, and a pair of rubber gloves for the less dangerous.

2 Hold the plant firmly, gently tip it into a horizontal position and slip it out of the old pot. Plastic pots may stick to the roots; if so, give a few thumps to the base of the pot to help free the plant.

3 Plants in clay pots can often be freed by pushing through the hole in the bottom; if this is unsuccessful, the soil will need loosening from the inside of the pot with a knife.

4 With the plant in a horizontal position, carefully loosen the root ball (roots) and remove as much of the old potting soil as possible. This is particularly important if you will be using a different type of potting soil, for example changing from or to a peat-based or soil-based potting soil.

5 Position the plant in its new container and see how much potting soil is required under the plant so that it will sit at the same height as before. Next, remove the plant and add the potting soil.

6 Finally, reposition the plant and carefully tip in more potting soil around it, firming gently as you go.

7 Fill the container to within about 1–2cm (¾in) of the top, and top-dress with gravel. Do not water for a couple of days, to allow any damaged roots to callus.

CHOOSING A CONTAINER TO SUIT YOUR PLANT

When repotting, there is a wide choice of containers on the market, from conventional flower pots and pans to bonsai bowls and decorative ceramic containers. For the greenhouse, conventional pots and pans are usually best; the size and shape will be determined by the plant size and habit. Tall plants will need full-depth pots; short or bushy succulent species will probably grow best in shallow pans. Some of the more bushy succulents can be grown in shallow bonsai pots and their growth restricted.

For growing plants indoors, more ornate containers can be used. Choose the colour with care: natural, earthy colours are usually best. Many brighter green, red or orange containers seem to clash with the plants and make them appear a peculiar colour.

Pots with drainage holes are much better for the plants, but if these are lacking, put a layer of gravel in the bottom of the container and put the plant in another pot inside it to allow drainage of surplus moisture.

Propagation in the wild

Succulents come from a wide range of different habitats and have developed a great number of ways to ensure successful propagation.

Many succulents have thick, swollen leaves to store moisture during drought periods, which are easily detached by wildlife brushing against them. Often the leaves have buds attached and, if left undisturbed, the buds will soon sprout to make new plants.

Plants in the Euphorbiaceae family have small, three-chambered seedpods which, when they dry, split open with great force, exploding their seeds over a wide area.

The plants of the Asclepiad family, such as *Hoya* and *Stapelia*, make long, twin-horned seedpods. These have a groove down one side; when they are ripe, they split open. The wide, flat, papery seeds have a cluster of long, fine hairs at the end which act like a parachute. As soon as there is a breath of wind, the seeds blow away from the parent, and so are distributed. *Senecio* and *Kleinia* also have small seeds with parachutes.

Aloe and its close relatives have tall flower stems which produce short, erect, sausage-shaped seedpods. When these are ripe, the three long seed chambers split down the sides

■ LEFT
Plants of the *Kalanchoe* genus, (syn. *Bryophyllum*) make new plantlets from the edges of the leaves. These minute new plants seem remarkably robust, and can be knocked off intact by passing animals or even a strong breeze. Most will take root where they fall, and often make very large colonies.

■ ABOVE
Echeveria flowers.

■ RIGHT
Echeveria flower stems.

Mesembryanthemum ripe, dry seedpod.

Mesembryanthemum seedpod that has opened shortly after watering.

from the tip. When the wind blows, the heads are shaken and the light seed is blown about.

Most members of the Crassulaceae family produce very fine seed which, when ripe, is also easily scattered by the wind. In many desert areas the ground is hard and undisturbed, and the small seeds can be blown along until they fall into a nook or cranny. These plants produce thousands of seeds, and some are sure to find a suitable new habitat.

The Aizoaceae family bears fruits that are like small, woody buttons which have numerous chambers. When they are ripe and come in contact with moisture, they rapidly expand to a star-like shape and expose some of their seeds. Heavy rain will wash some seeds from the capsule. As the fruit dries again, it will close and wait for further rain before repeating the process.

The minute seeds are often viable for up to 10–20 years.

Not many succulents have large succulent fruits, except perhaps the cucumber family. These are usually harvested by indigenous wildlife as food, and often the seeds are a waste product. Some birds, for example, eat the fleshy fruit and distribute the seeds in their excrement.

Aloe flowers.

Aloe seedpod, left, and flower, right.

Propagation by seeds

Succulents are mostly easy plants to propagate, whether from seed or by cuttings. Each method has its place and, with a little practice, can easily be used to increase the size of any plant collection.

Taking cuttings will produce quicker results, but if you have the patience, growing plants from seed can give a great sense of satisfaction, and is an easy way to add many new varieties to your collection.

Some, particularly the Aizoaceae and Liliaceae families, easily set seed, which can be harvested to grow more plants. Plants of the Crassulaceae family mostly have very small, dust-like seed, and viability can be quite short (six months) and very unreliable: the seeds germinate either in vast numbers or at a rate of 1–2 per cent. These plants are therefore usually grown from cuttings.

Some other groups rarely make viable seed in cultivation, often because more than one plant is needed to cross-fertilize them. The Asclepiad group (*Stapelia*, *Hoya*, *Stephanotis*) have peculiar pollinating mechanisms that require specific insects to pollinate them: it is extremely difficult to do this by hand.

Seed of many succulents is available through specialist seed suppliers and plant societies. The more common species, particularly the hardy ones such as *Sedum*, are usually much easier to obtain from general gardening outlets.

Seed raising

It is best to sow seed in a heated propagator in late winter, so that the seedlings can grow as large as possible before the following winter. If you do not have a propagator, wait until the weather warms up in late spring/

RAISING SUCCULENTS BY SEED

1 Begin by filling a small pot with potting soil, and press down with your fingers until it feels firm.

2 Scatter the seed carefully and evenly over the surface of the potting soil.

3 Cover the pot with fine gravel. Water well and place in a warm, bright but shady position.

■ BELOW
Seedlings have very delicate, fine roots, and these can be easily damaged.

early summer before sowing. Some winter-growing succulents such as *Lewisia* and *Lithops* will often germinate better at the beginning of their growing season in early autumn.

Fifty seeds can be sown comfortably in an 8cm (3in) pot or 1,000 into a standard seed tray. Sowing different kinds of seeds in individual pots or containers is better, as it allows for the differing germination rates between species.

When the seeds have germinated, they will grow well under normal greenhouse conditions with a minimum temperature of 10°C

(50°F). If left in the propagator, it should be well ventilated, or the warm, humid environment that results could lead to a fatal attack of damping off. The young seedlings should be protected from direct, strong sunlight.

Normal seed trays are quite shallow and should be completely filled with potting soil, so that they hold enough soil and moisture and ensure a good growth rate. Seedlings should be watered regularly when they are dry, and the addition of a cactus fertilizer will speed up growth rates.

4 Provided the seedlings are not too dense, leave them undisturbed until they are large enough to pot individually, which may take from three months to two years.

5 When repotting the seedlings, dig them up carefully, avoiding handling them by the delicate roots.

6 Succulent seedlings are never uniform in their growth rate, and there will be a variety of sizes in each batch. The larger seedlings can be potted individually; the smaller replanted in rows in a seed tray.

Propagation by cuttings

Taking cuttings can be a very easy and rewarding method of propagating succulents. There are three main types of cutting: leaf, stem and root.

Leaf cuttings

Many of the Crassulaceae family can be propagated from leaf cuttings. Leaves can be detached from the stems complete with their axillary bud, which may or may not be visible. If the leaf detaches easily, the bud will normally be attached to it. This is a particularly useful way to propagate rosette plants such as *Echeveria*.

Where the leaves will not detach easily from the rosette, wait until flowering time and then use the leaves from the flowering stem. An ideal time for this type of propagation is during spring and summer. At other times of year, a bottom heat of 21–27°C (70–80°F) will speed up the rooting process.

Stem cuttings

Two main groups of succulents are suitable for propagation by means of stem cuttings: those which have thickened and swollen stems, and the more leafy plants.

Many succulents are bushy, shrubby or make ground-cover plants without having swollen stems. Instead, the stems can be normal leafy stems, rosette-forming or almost stemless rosettes of tight-packed, swollen leaves.

The cutting length will depend on the species, but an ideal length for many leafy plants is 5–8cm (2–3in), because longer cuttings tend to collapse under their own weight as they dehydrate while rooting. The length of stem on the more highly succulent, swollen stems will depend on the species. It should be long enough

RAISING SUCCULENTS BY LEAF CUTTINGS

1 The easiest way to remove the leaf and axillary bud is by gently pushing a mature, but not shrivelled, leaf sideways. Allow the leaves to dry for a day or so.

2 If a number of leaves are being used, use a seed tray. If just one or two leaves, use a small pot. Fill with gritty cactus potting soil and top up with a thin layer of fine grit. Push the leaves into the gravel so that they will stand up, and are thus less likely to rot.

3 Lightly water occasionally so that the potting soil is kept slightly damp, and the leaves will normally root in two to six weeks. After six months, there should be considerable growth and the new plants will be ready for potting on.

to allow you to push about 1cm (½in) into the gravel. Where the plants make clustering rosettes, they should be detached at their base, and a few bottom leaves removed to expose 1cm (½in) of stem. Plants that make tall stem rosettes can be cut at a suitable height to make a new plant.

If a number of cuttings are being raised at the same time, use a seed tray or a shallow, suitably sized container. Three-quarters fill it with a free-draining, gritty potting soil and then top up with a layer of fine grit. After the cuttings have callused for a couple of days, push them into the gravel, sufficiently far for them to stand up. Water the container or tray from time to time to keep the potting soil just slightly damp. Cuttings will normally root in three to six weeks. An ideal time of year is from spring until early autumn. At other times of the year some bottom heat may be required. High humidity will soon rot the cuttings – if a propagator is used, it is best left open or at least well ventilated. When the cuttings have rooted, they can be potted up and treated normally for the species.

Root cuttings

A few species can be propagated by root cuttings. Certain plants produce underground growths which are either stolons, stems or roots, from which new plants grow. This is particularly useful in groups such as *Agave*, *Sansevieria* and *Pelargonium*.

Certain groups of plants (*Ceropegia*, *Pelargonium* and some *Kleinia*) make underground storage organs or tubers. They can be detached and potted, and normally develop into new plants.

PROPAGATION BY CUTTINGS FROM SWOLLEN OR THICKENED STEMS

1 Cut the stem to a suitable length – if too long, it will probably bend and twist during the rooting process. Stems less than about 2.5cm (1in) will probably be very slow to make new plants, unless all the proportions of the plant are small. Allow the cutting to callus for a few days before planting.

2 Use a small pot that is large enough to take the cutting, and keep it upright. Fill the pot about three-quarters full of potting soil and cover with a thin layer of fine grit. Stand the cutting on the grit and top up with fine gravel. Allow to stand for a few days and then water lightly, and repeat occasionally.

3 When active new growth is seen, gently tip the pot on its side and pour out the gravel. If the cutting has rooted, replace the grit with gritty soil; if not, replace the gravel and wait a while. Initially, be a little sparing with water until it is well established. When it is growing well, repot into a normal-size container.

Division

There are many succulents (*Haworthia*, *Gasteria* and *Aloe*) which produce basal offsets. Many of the Crassulaceae family (*Crassula* and *Sedum*) make clumps, and the stems and offsets root freely while still attached to the parent.

General tips

Most normal gardening practices hold for succulents. However, remember that these plants need less water than garden plants, and normally will not tolerate very low temperatures. Use a gritty potting soil to help prevent waterlogging, and top-dress with grit to keep the leaves away from damp, cold soil. Usually the time it takes for a cutting to root will be dictated by the temperature and moisture levels. Keep rooting cuttings out of full sun so that they do not dehydrate quicker than they can root.

Remember to take several cuttings if material is available, as this improves the chances of producing a new plant. It is always worth trying to grow something of which you are unsure or is difficult, as the chances are that you will succeed and gain great satisfaction in the process.

SEPARATING NEW UNDERGROUND STEMS

1 In groups where underground stems grow into new plants *(Agave* and *Sansevieria)*, they are best left attached to the parent plant until they have developed a complete circle of leaves. At this point, remove the adult plant from its pot and tease away the new plant from the parent.

2 Trim away any surplus underground stem. An independent root system will have developed, and the new plant can be potted up after a couple of days when any cut or damaged tissue has callused.

PROPAGATION THROUGH DIVISION

1 Lift parent plant and offsets from the pot, and carefully pull the latter apart into single heads or clumps, as desired.

2 Pot up rooted pieces to make instant plants. Unrooted sections can be treated as cuttings and can be planted in seed trays until they take root.

Pests and diseases

Given reasonable cultivation, succulents are not particularly prone to pests and diseases. Most insecticides and fungicides used for normal plants can readily be used on most succulents. However, do read and follow the instructions for their use.

Mealy bug

How to identify: It is like a small, white woodlouse with a very waxy coating. It is more often first spotted because of its nests, which are like little blobs of cotton wool. When crushed, the small mealy bug is bright red (it is the source for the dye cochineal). This is perhaps the worst pest to attack succulents and cacti. There are many different types of mealy bug, often associated with different kinds of host plant. Most found on indoor plants seem to enjoy succulents as a host plant.
Cause: Most pests, including mealy bug, are introduced from other infected plants.
Control and prevention: The best cure is to treat with a systemic insecticide that is absorbed by the plant and poisons its sap. When the pests feed, they are killed. Adding a little soap or wetting agent to a contact poison will help to penetrate the insects' waxy coat.

Red spider mite

How to identify: This minute insect is more brown than red, and is about the size of finely ground white pepper. It is hardly visible to the naked eye, and the first signs are usually a very fine but dense web, or the growing point of the plant turning brown – this gradually spreads down the plant body. It is particularly noticeable on the softer-skinned plants.
Cause: Plants are most likely to become infected by contact with other plants.
Control and prevention: Regular spraying with insecticide that is also a miticide will control it.

Mealy bug insect.

Usually the first sign of red spider mite is the fine dense web that forms on the plant.

Diseases

How to identify: Most of the diseases that succulents suffer from are usually caused by being too wet and/or too cold. Young plants, particularly seedlings, are prone to damping off if too wet. Treating with a copper-based fungicide like Cheshunt compound will control or prevent this problem.
Cause: Rotting from a plant's base usually indicates over-watering, particularly when the plant is dormant. This normally occurs in cool conditions, but can also happen during hot weather when plants may become dormant to conserve moisture.

Rotting from the top of a plant is often a sign of cold damage, especially if exposed to frosts. Also, tender new growth can scorch if plants are moved from a shady position into full sun, or if there is a sudden change in weather from a long dark spell to brilliant sun.
Control and prevention: The rotting parts of larger plants should be cut out as soon as possible with a sharp knife, and discarded. The tissue should be cut back so that there is no sign of discoloration, or the rot will probably continue through the plant. The cut surfaces can either be left exposed to the air, if warm and dry, or treated with green sulphur.

During winter in cooler climates, there is usually a very high humidity, and plants in a greenhouse or other confined space will greatly benefit from circulating air. If this is not possible, the temperature will need to be a few degrees higher to prevent damping off. Dying, decaying or rotting leaves should be removed immediately and discarded, and an eye kept on the plant. In most cases, correcting the growing conditions will prevent most of these problems.

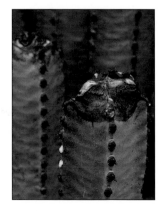

Crown that has died back due to cold damage.

Calendar

Spring

Repot any plants that have outgrown their containers, and any that have not been repotted for a long time. Wait a few days after repotting before watering. On warm, bright, sunny days encourage the plants back into growth by the occasional light watering or spray. Sow seeds in a heated propagator. As the weather improves, water occasionally until active new growth can be seen. As soon as the plants are growing, again commence regular watering, and fertilize about once a week. Allow the potting soil to dry out thoroughly before watering again.

■ ABOVE
Faucaria tigrina

Summer

Finish repotting anything left over from the spring that still needs repotting. Sow seeds on a windowsill or in a greenhouse. Take cuttings and allow to callus. Remove germinated seedlings from the propagator to harden off, and make room to sow some more. Pot callused cuttings into a gritty potting soil. Keep an eye open for pests and diseases, and treat accordingly. Water and feed plants when they are dry. Slightly ease off watering the more mature desert plants, as many will become almost dormant in the height of summer. Keep seedlings shaded from the full sun, as they are prone to scorch.

Autumn

Begin to ease off watering, and stop feeding to give the new growth a chance to ripen before winter. As the days become shorter and the nights colder, pots take very much longer to dry out. Treat all plants with an insecticide so that they are pest-free for the winter.

Early winter

Put the summer-growing plants to rest until the spring, and tail off watering completely. The winter-

■ ABOVE
Aeonium arboreum atropurpureum

growing species should be watered sparingly, as pots dry very slowly at this time of year. Check heaters and make sure that they work and are ready when needed. Examine the plants regularly for any disease so that problems can be sorted out before they take a hold.

Mid-winter

Keep a regular check on plants to make sure that there are no signs of rot or disease. Check the heating daily to make sure it is working. Ventilate on warm, bright, sunny days. Plan the coming year. Order seeds.

Other recommended succulents

Agave americana variegata

These are the different genera of succulent plants most likely to be encountered by collectors (apart from those listed in the Plant Directory). New plants are being discovered all the time, and the list is almost endless. In addition, some genera, such as *Sedum* and *Stapelia*, have had major reviews and been split into many new genera. These new names are likely to be encountered only in highly specialized publications, until they either gain wider acceptance or are changed again.

Adenia (Passifloraceae)
These large, caudex-forming plants produce branches from the caudex. They have cream to yellow flowers and attractive, globular to plumshaped fruit. Challenging to grow. Minimum temperature 10°C (50°F).

Adenium (**Apocynaceae**)
Spineless, caudex-bearing plants with very attractive flowers. On some species the caudex can be half-buried; in others it is tree-like. Good house plants. Minimum temperature 15°C (60°F).
Adromischus (**Crassulaceae**)
Small, clumping to spreading plants mostly with thick, swollen leaves, attractively marked. The flowers are funnel-shaped, white to pink, on long, slender, terminal stems. Minimum temperature 5°C (42°F).
Agave americana variegata
Differs from *A. mediopicta alba* in that the leaves have a yellow edge, not a central pale stripe. Makes a fine, large plant, but can be contained in a pot to restrict growth. Minimum temperature 5°C (42°F)
Aloinopsis (**Aizoaceae**) See also *Nananthus*. Small, thick-leafed, rosette succulents, often with tuberous roots. Flowers are small and daisy-like, usually with a reddish stripe. Summer-dormant, it grows in spring and autumn. Minimum temperature 5°C (42°F) if dry.
Anacampseros (**Portulaceae**)
This group has recently been split into two parts, *Anacampseros* for the succulent leafy species and *Avonia* for those producing

Bowiea volubilis

many papery sheaths that cover the small leaves. The former are mostly small plants with small, succulent leaves. Minimum temperature 5°C (42°F).
Argyroderma (**Aizoaceae**) In the wild these small succulent plants are almost white, but in cultivation they are white-green or white-blue. The plant is composed of a swollen pair of leaves like an egg split across the middle. The flowers appear in autumn. Minimum temperature 5°C (42°F) if dry.
Bowiea (**Hyacinthaceae**)
These underground, bulbous species produce one leaf annually followed by a long, climbing inflorescence. This can grow many yards long, resembling a multi-branched string.Small, greenish flowers appear in autumn. Minimum temperature 5°C (42°F).

Brachystelma
(**Asclepiadaceae**) Annual stems appear from tubers. Some species have fairly short stems, others long, slender, climbing or creeping stems. The small, star-like, summer flowers can be foul smelling. Awkward and difficult plants, they are best left to the specialist. Minimum temperature 10°C (50°F).
Cephalophyllum (**Aizoaceae**)
Clump-forming or carpeting plants producing bright, daisy-like flowers. Minimum temperature 5°C (42°F).
Ceropegia (**Asclepiadaceae**)
A large group of mostly climbing plants, some leafy, some almost leafless, with unusual flowers. Some are small, tuberous plants; others have thick, fleshy roots. Minimum temperature 5–15°C (42–60°F).
Ceropegia stapeliiformis
The creeping, arching or pendent, almost leafless stems are green to grey-green, and often blotched. The unusual flowers can vary between plants in shape and colour. Comparatively easy to grow and flower. Minimum temperature 7°C (45°F).
Ceropegia woodii (**of cultivation**) The plant produces tubers along the length of its stem at the internodes, where they are in contact with the soil.

The unusual, dark, lantern-like flowers appear throughout the year. A good house plant. Minimum temperature 5°C (42°F).

Cissus (Vitaceae) Diverse group with some succulent species. Most are climbing plants, often with swollen stems. Minimum temperature 10–15°C (50–60°F).

Conophytum minutum As this species is widespread in the wild, it is very variable both as to head size and markings. The flowers are shaded white to magenta. Minimum temperature 5°C (42°F).

Conophytum tantalinum f. eenkokerense The very small heads of this plant are distinctive with their wide fissure and 'eared' shape. Flowers magenta to pink. Minimum temperature 5°C (42°F).

Crassula arborescens This larger-growing species will eventually grow to 3m (10ft) or more high. It is comparatively slow-growing, and the leaves and branches are very heavy, usually leading to slightly pendent branches on older plants. Larger plants will produce clusters of pink flowers.

Cyphostemma (Vitaceae) Originally classified as *Cissus*, this group has been separated because of its large, swollen, caudex-like trunks. They

Conophytum minutum

produce annual leaves and, in the main, are slow-growing. Not particularly easy to cultivate. Minimum temperature 10°C (50°F).

Delosperma (Aizoaceae) Small, bush-forming, clumping or carpeting plants producing many daisy-like flowers, often in bright colours. Minimum temperature 3°C (38°F).

Dioscorea (Dioscoraceae) Tuber-forming plants producing annual climbing vines. Very similar to *Testudinaria*. Minimum temperature 10°C (50°F).

Dischidia (Asclepiadaceae) Very similar to *Hoya* but with different floral characteristics. Most are more slender-stemmed and not easy to grow. Minimum temperature 10°C (50°F).

Dorstenia (Moraceae) These members of the fig family are mostly small-growing, and

have swollen roots or bases. The unusual 'flower' is like a small, opened fig with many minute flowers on it. One for the specialist. Minimum temperature 10°C (50°F).

Drosanthemum (Aizoaceae) Carpeting plants or small bushes. Ideal for outdoor cultivation in frost-free areas. Mostly free-flowering, they produce small, daisy-like flowers in a variety of colours. Minimum temperature 4°C (38°F).

Echeveria nodulosa An attractive, bushy species with dark maroon markings on its deep olive-green leaves. The tall flower stems with deep reddish flowers appear in summer. Look out for the hybrid/cultivar 'Painted Lady'. Minimum temperature 5°C (42°F).

Euphorbia canariensis As the name suggests, this plant is from the Canary Islands. Of medium height, with great age it will make large clumps. When larger, the stems of this species produce many purple flowers from the upper parts of the stem. Liable to red spider mite damage. Minimum temperature 7°C (45°F).

Fouquieria (Fouquieriaceae) Although these plants, known as Ocotillo, are plentiful in the wild, they are not easy in cultivation. The plants grow in short cycles, when moisture

Crassula arborescens

is available, each lasting a few weeks. Minimum temperature 10°C (50°F).

Gasteria nitida armstrongii One of the neater and more compact members of this genus, with its tongue-like, dark leaves. Plants can vary enormously in size and colour, but all are attractive. Larger specimens soon offset to make large clumps. The flower spikes appear in spring. Minimum temperature 2°C (35°F).

Gasteria verruculosa This distinctive species has long, narrow leaves, arranged in a fan shape, covered in raised, white dots. Plants grow easily and soon make clumps. Minimum temperature 2°C (35°F).

Gerardanthus (Cucurbitaceae) A large, caudex-forming plant that produces a rapid-growing annual vine with silvery green, ivy-shaped leaves. The cucumber-like fruit are hollow, and the three basal flaps open when ripe so that the seeds can drop out. Minimum temperature 10°C (50°F).

Gibbaeum (**Aizoaceae**) Small, clump-forming plants with thick, fleshy leaves, mostly with one of the pair shorter than the other, the long one slightly hooked at the end. Mostly spring- or autumn-flowering. Easy. Minimum temperature 4°C (40°F).

Glottiphyllum (**Aizoaceae**) Small, clumping plants, the stems with pairs of dense, thick, fleshy, green leaves lying flat on the ground. The bright yellow flowers appear from summer to autumn. Best grown in poor soil to restrict growth. Minimum temperature 5°C (42°F).

Glottiphyllum nelii Difficult to identify, this is a small-growing species, and suitable for small spaces. Minimum temperature 5°C (42°F).

Graptopetalum (**Crassulaceae**) Like *Echeveria*, but with different floral characteristics. Minimum temperature 5°C (42°F).

Graptopetalum bellum Originally called *Tacitus bellus*. The tight-packed rosettes of small, grey-brown to green leaves make ideal hiding places for pests,

Glottiphyllum nelii

particularly mealy bugs, and are also good at trapping moisture, making them quite prone to rotting at low temperatures. Minimum temperature 10°C (50°F).

Greenovia (**Crassulaceae**) Very closely related to *Aeonium*. The rosettes are normally almost stemless. Minimum temperature 4°C (38°F).

Haworthia cuspidata The broad, pale green leaves of this species are quite distinctive. Plants offset freely to make large domed clumps. Minimum temperature 5°C (42°F).

Haworthia reinwardtii **v. *chalumnensis*** This is one of the few species that becomes columnar, the stems surrounded by tight packed leaves. Grown in full sun in summer with little water, the stems turn deep red, although the leaves are liable to shrivel

if too warm and dry. Kept in slight shade in summer will give a more attractive plant, but sadly lacking the red colour. Minimum temperature 5°C (42°F).

Hesperaloe (**Agavaceae**) A semi-hardy, green rosette with long, stiff, green leaves. Plants clump with age. They resemble some kinds of *Agave* and *Yucca*. Minimum temperature 3°C (38°F).

Hoya carnosa One of the easiest succulent hoyas to grow, this is widely cultivated as a house plant. A vigorous climber that prefers shade, it will survive 5°C (42°F) in winter, but grows better at 10°C (50°F).

Jatropha (**Euphorbiaceae**) Many species have a swollen tuber or stem, producing annual growths. The flowers of the more common species are orange-red. Moderately difficult, mostly requiring 10°C (50°F) in winter.

Kedrostris (**Cucurbitaceae**) Most produce rapid-growing annual vines and small flowers. This genus is fairly easy to grow and will produce a large caudex, saucer-like or like a swollen hand, mostly buried. Minimum temperature 7°C (45°F).

Kleinia articulatus The short cylindrical or knobbly stems of this plant are capped in autumn and winter with a head of

Jatropha podagrica

greenish-purple leaves. If this species is grown in rich soil, with plenty of food and water, the plants will produce long, brittle stems. The clusters of foul-smelling, small, yellowish flowers appear in the autumn. Minimum temperature 5°C (42°F).

Kleinia rowleyana (**String of Beads**) The beauty of this plant is its swollen, pea-like leaves on long, slender stems. Grown in a hanging pot they have the effect of a bead curtain. Although it will rot if kept permanently wet, it does require more water than many other succulents. The small, almost insignificant flowers appear in autumn and are sweetly perfumed. Minimum temperature 5°C (42°F).

Malephora (**Aizoaceae**) Shrubby plants, mostly with bluish cylindrical leaves and small, yellow flowers. Minimum temperature 5°C (42°F).

Nananthus schoonesii

Momordica (Cucurbitaceae)
These plants have swollen bases and produce annual, rapid-growing, climbing stems. Minimum temperature 10°C (50°F).

Monadenium
(Euphorbiaceae) Mostly small, bushy plants with small, succulent leaves and thickened, fleshy, green stems, sometimes thorny. The 'flowers' are usually small and pale, shaped like a bonnet (hooded). Ideal for a windowsill. Minimum temperature 10°C (50°F).

Nananthus **(Aizoaceae)**
Small, clumping or mounding, almost stemless plants with thickened, fleshy leaves. Most have a swollen root stock. The small, daisy-like flowers are produced in autumn and spring. Very sensitive to overwatering. Minimum temperature 7°C (45°F) if dry.

Nolina **(Agavaceae)** These plants have swollen bases and grass-like leaves. The best known is the pony tail palm which has a large, swollen trunk topped with a large rosette. Easy to grow, they require moderate watering in summer. Minimum temperature 7°C (45°F).

Othonna **(Asteraceae)** A strange group of mostly small, tuberous or swollen-stemmed plants producing leaves for a short period in autumn and/or winter. Most have small, yellow, daisy-like flowers. They are not easy to grow. Minimum temperature 10°C (50°F).

Pachyphytum **(Crassulaceae)** A group of rosette succulents related to *Echeveria* with which they hybridize quite easily. The leaves are often more cylindrical than flat. Most can be propagated quite easily from leaves. Minimum temperature 5°C (42°F).

Pachyphytum oviferum
The common name, sugared almond plant, describes the leaf shape exactly. The rosettes of powdery blue to pink leaves send up flower spikes during early summer, which, from above, are almost the same colour as the leaves. The pendent flowers have bright red petals. Good for a hanging basket. Minimum temperature 7°C (45°F).

Pachyphytum oviferum

Pedilanthus **(Euphorbiaceae)** A small group of bushy succulents with swollen stems and few leaves. The small flowers are beak-like. The sap is poisonous in all species. Minimum temperature 10°C (50°F).

Pelargonium carnosum The plants tend to be summer-growing, shedding their foliage in the autumn to leave just the swollen, bare stems which can be up to 60cm (2ft) tall. The flowers appear from spring to autumn. Prone to rotting. Minimum temperature 5°C (42°F).

Plumeria **(Apocynaceae)** Large-growing bushes, known as frangipani, producing fragrant flowers in summer. Plants grown in small greenhouses are disappointing; much more suitable for garden culture in warm climates. Minimum temperature 10°C (50°F).

Portulacaria afra v. *variegata* This variegated form tends to be slower growing and more compact than the green forms, but is ideal as a house plant. Minimum temperature 7°C (45°F).

Pterodiscus **(Pedaliceae)** Small, caudex plants making short stems, and flowering during the summer. Plants are prone to rotting if overwet or cold. Difficult. Minimum temperature 10°C (50°F).

Pyrenacantha **(Icacinaceae)** These plants make large, boulder-like caudexes and produce semi-succulent, annual, climbing stems. Seldom seen in cultivation. Minimum temperature 10°C (50°F).

Rhodiola **(Crassulaceae)** A sub-group of *Sedum*.

Ruschia **(Aizoaceae)** Small to medium-sized bushes, clumping or trailing plants. Most have small, bright, daisy-like flowers. A diverse group from which many smaller groups have been extracted. Minimum temperature 4°C (39°F).

Sansevieria **(Dracaenaceae)** Sometimes called mother-in-law's tongue, these well-known house plants come from mostly hot, dry areas. There are a number of different species, mostly with spear-shaped leaves. Minimum temperature 10°C (50°F).

Stapelia leendertziae

Sarcocaulon (**Geraniaceae**)
These strange plants come from dry, desert areas, and for a large part of the year resemble dead twigs. In the wild, when conditions are favourable, they can come into leaf, flower, set seed and ripen in four to six weeks. Awkward and difficult plants, best left to the specialist. Minimum temperature 10°C (50°F).

Sarcostemma
(**Asclepiadaceae**) Climbing, slender-stemmed, almost leafless plants. They produce small, star-like flowers under ideal growing conditions. Uninteresting as small plants. Minimum temperature 10°C (50°F).

Sempervivum (**Crassulaceae**)
These mostly European plants are hardy alpines forming compact rosettes. In different locations the plants will adopt slightly different forms,

making identification extremely difficult. Most produce pink or red flowers on tall stems. Hardy. Minimum temperature 4°C (25°F).

Senecio (**Asteraceae**) See also *Kleinia*. Mostly small to medium-sized bushes producing compound flowers surrounded by yellow ray florets (like petals). Very diverse group. Minimum temperature 5°C (42°F).

Senecio haworthii The white to silvery, pointed, cylindrical leaves are covered in a dense mat of tiny hairs. The plants branch freely to make small bushes, although they seldom flower as small plants in pots. Minimum temperature 5°C (42°F).

Stapelia (**Asclepiadaceae**)
This large family of plants is difficult to cultivate and keep in good condition. It contains over 700 species in a large number of different genera. The plants mainly have small, finger-like stems and produce small to large, star-shaped flowers, many quite evil-smelling. Minimum temperature 10°C (50°F).

Stapelia leendertziae Perhaps one of the easier, larger-growing members of this group. The large, dark, cup-like flowers appear during summer. Minimum temperature 10°C (50°F).

Uncarina decaryi

Stomatium (**Aizoaceae**)
Small, carpeting plants, mostly with short, chunky leaves with 'toothed' edges arranged in small rosettes. Small yellow or white flowers appear in summer and autumn. Minimum temperature 7°C (45°F).

Synadenium (**Euphorbiaceae**)
A large bush with thickened leaves, sometimes sold as a house plant. The sap is poisonous and can cause painful blistering. Minimum temperature 10°C (50°F).

Trichodiadema (**Aizoaceae**)
Small, bushy or sprawling plants with short, cylindrical leaves, usually with a tuft of short hairs at their end. Most are easy to grow. Minimum temperature 5°C (42°F).

Tylecodon (**Crassulaceae**)
Tylecodon is an anagram of *Cotyledon*, the genus where these plants used to be classified. They were

separated because of their swollen stems, winter growth and mostly deciduous habit. Many are small-growing, clumping plants, but a few species are larger-growing bushes. Minimum temperature 10°C (50°F).

Tylecodon paniculata
This large, bush-like species has papery, golden-brown bark which gives rise to its common name, butter tree. It is winter-growing, starting into growth in early autumn and shedding its leaves in spring before flowering. Minimum temperature 7°C (45°F).

Tylecodon schaeferana This small-growing species has a tuberous root and numerous, very short stems. The small, sausage-shaped leaves appear in autumn after the small, pink, cup-like flowers. An interesting plant, dormant during summer. Minimum temperature 9°C (48°F).

Uncarina (**Pedaliceae**) A small group of tropical trees and shrubs with beautiful flowers. Most require a high temperature and are best left to the specialist. Minimum temperature 12°C (54°F).

Xerosicyos (**Cucurbitaceae**)
A small group of climbing, tendril-bearing plants from Madagascar. Small flowers. Minimum temperature 12°C (54°F).

Index

ACKNOWLEDGEMENTS
The publisher would like to thank the following people for their help in the production of this book: Hollygate Cactus Nursery, West Sussex, UK; and Miles Anderson, Arizona, USA.

Echeveria 'Frosty'